Fergus Allen was born in London of an Irish father and an English mother. He grew up in Ireland, attending Quaker schools in Dublin and Waterford. Since graduating in civil engineering from Trinity College, Dublin, he has lived and worked in England, where much of his career has been in the Civil Service. Having been Director of Hydraulics Research, he moved to the Cabinet Office and subsequently became First Civil Service Commissioner. He is married, with two daughters, and lives in Berkshire.

FERGUS ALLEN

The Brown Parrots
of Providencia

faber and faber
LONDON · BOSTON

First published in 1993
by Faber and Faber Limited
3 Queen Square London WC1N 3AU

Photoset by Wilmaset Ltd, Wirral
Printed by Clays Ltd, St Ives plc

© Fergus Allen, 1993

A CIP record for this book is available from the British Library

ISBN 0-571-17011-0

2 4 6 8 10 9 7 5 3 1

To Joan

Acknowledgements

My thanks are due to the editors of the following magazines, in which a number of these poems first appeared: *The Atlantic Monthly, English, Envoi, Irish Times, Listen, London Magazine, New Statesman, Poetry Ireland Review, The Rialto, Times Literary Supplement*; and to the publishers of the following anthologies: *Beyond the Shore, The Guinness Book of Poetry, Springtime, Penguin Book of Yet More Comic and Curious Verse.*

Contents

I

Other   3
Tanks in Moscow   4
The Brown Parrots of Providencia   5
Forestry   6
Songs of Irish Innocence   7
Foreign Relations   8
Actor in Mirror   9
A History of Philosophy   10
Looking over London   11
On Top   12
Firing   14
Not for Transcription into Braille   15
From the North   16
Shopping   18
Necropolis   19
Sodium Light   20
Prayer-wheel   21
Aside   22
Thoughts Slide out of Thoughts   23
Wall of Death, Bray   24
History   25
Flies and Nettles   26
Big Cat   27
Montages   28
In Hartslock Wood   29
What the Wild Waves Say   30
Genealogy   31
Pantomime   33

A Samaritan Surprised   34
Sleep   37
Konzertstück   38
Revelations   39
Country and Town   40
Reading Time   41

II

A Tropical Caress   45
Descending   46
Is There Life on Venus?   47
A Suit of Armour   48
The Musical Lover   49
Kostchei   51
Elegy for Faustina   52
The Assassination   53
Townsman in the Country   54
First-born   55
In the Tower   56
The Exile   57
The Seven Banquets   59
A Meeting on Gold Leaf   61

III

The Fall   65

I

Other

As against the odds as the mating of dugong –
A figure of speech for the all-but-unthinkable.
Just one skin-quivering horse tests my credulity,
A discrete entity without hands or wings
Standing there in a field, not plugged into anything.
It lives on stage in a quite different play.

I can believe in a world of vegetation,
Weather and mechanical insects, but flinch
When our black cat, *Felis catus*, stands revealed
As a foreign body elbow deep in meadow,
Weighing me up with his incurious eyes –
The slits of an armoured car would show more interest.

This is the familiar that an hour ago
Flatteringly weaved and purred around my ankles;
Now, among buttercups and timothy-grass,
He might have descended from a flying saucer –
Alien as the peacock on our bathroom roof
Screaming challenges from the time of the dinosaurs.

I, too, clad in bits and pieces like a caddis,
Can feel more than a little extraterrestrial,
And naked in a field would look even odder
Than horse or cat, whose unspeculative stares
Assess me as food or threat, not as philosopher
Reckoning up the things in heaven and earth.

Tanks in Moscow

Men push bare-armed against an iron chin
Inching forward down Kalinin Prospect.
Might as well be pushing against an iceberg.
Hands haul a mate from under teeth of tracks
About to consume him. (*Cut to next picture.*)

A woman is beating on the armour-plate;
It smashes under her fists like an eggshell.
Inside are soldiers with wet feathers and big eyes,
Curled up, unready to be hatched on to the world.
She screams at their dazed uncomprehending faces.

On television screens we observe her passion
While we eat scrambled egg or sip gin-and-tonic
Or get up to open the door for the cat
Who has seen it all before and has in mind
Small mammals that come to the pond at nightfall.

The Brown Parrots of Providencia

Money from hamburgers helped regild
The rococo theatre where a renowned
Ballerina, after a *pas de deux*
And the pathos of shivering arms,
Tilts forward on one foot and delicately
Exposes her crotch.
                              From the esplanade,
On the margins of some holy festival,
See the brown parrots of Providencia
Fly shrieking from their wickerwork crates
Through a mist of salt, feathers whistling
And rattling, to the pinnate palms.
No inculcated lingo here; Polly
Tickles her palate with pebble tongue.

And see beneath the silk-cotton trees
All those bullet-shaped insects on their backs,
Waving their legs at the universe –
Creatures unnoticed in Unthank's popular
Guide to the Beetles of the New World.

Forestry

The tree-surgeon arrived on crutches,
Laid them down, flexed his tattooed biceps,
Squinted up at the dark-sailed sycamore,
Then, with ladder and rope and chainsaw
Screaming, rained down white-hearted logs,
Bombs with defective fuses, thudding
On soil channelled by worms and thronged
With startled insects, mites, bacteria.

On a kindling of tyres and gasoline
Piled-up leafy rubbish inflamed
With a whoosh and a bronchial roar;
It was orange day for the bystanders
From the world of spiders, who perished
In what to man appeared a twinkling.

Songs of Irish Innocence

Love walked right in, crossed the room and went out
By a door marked *Authorized Personnel Only*.
But I am not authorized, never was,
Never knew where the exeats came from,
Never liked to ask.

O the red red robin bob-bob-bobbed along;
But red I was told meant *stop*, so I stopped,
And green, when its turn came, came with a halo;
Traffic nosing through mist, *noli me tangere*
Beside the seaside.

Round the mulberry bush and folded hebe
And sticky escallonia, while the Kish lightship
Heaves at her moorings and groans of granite,
Run children, clasping hands that guide and distance,
Dancing in the fog.

Foreign Relations

Within the sum of words, there are words
From which we all, well, most of us,
Start back like a mangabey
From an exploding seed-pod.
But your name is my private bugaboo.

The insects are frying tonight.
During eternity in your bedroom
All those heavy-handed banana trees
Are standing around listlessly
In the so-called garden, waiting
For the fat grey rain and flickers
Of sheet lightning before dawn.

Worst of all is dinner at the Mangoro –
Your affected diction in public
And your pawnbroker's eyes.
My French is better than your English.
A psychic would see the boredom
Emanating from me as a violet aura.
No wonder the plants in this country
Are covered with spines and thorns.

But the unreeling time-machine
Says that my soul shall once again be gripped
By your soap-smooth thighs and wet lips.
Having you, my manganese-black idol,
I need not make to myself a graven image.

Actor in Mirror

Dark roles, my agent says they're me –
Iago, Bosola, Thersites
And specimens of today's manhood
From similar stables, assorted
Pimps, betrayers and glassy psychopaths.
Not for me the bravura villain
Or cool-headed amorous spy,
Only the kind you want to spit on.

When it's *She Stoops* or *The Importance*
The phone is silent, I perform
Light housework for ladies and gentlemen,
Repolishing their polished floors,
Searching in their watery pier-glasses
For the devil-face in the window.
But the flesh-coloured moon looks harmless –
Innocent eyes estimating innocence.

Yes, I know there's a hint of shark
In the overshot jaw and gliding
Gait, but not in the mind's construction.
Visit the whitewashed cells inside:
No spiders crouching or moulds fruiting
On these hygienic walls; Charles Kingsley
Can take a guided tour – and leave
A water baby if he wishes.

A History of Philosophy

Acting on advice, he carried a bundle of light,
Showing it on demand at halts in his night-time journey
And they allowed him to pass. Reaching his destination
He found himself known as swami, the teacher in white.

What he spoke without forethought was recorded, what
   he wore
Was touched, though none behaved any better or
   recovered
Nor was the juice of the roadside crab-tree any sweeter.
Some grew rich, but the poor remained as poor as before.

They gaped at his door and pressed after him down the
   street
And to each who approached he handed a brilliant fibre
Which doused itself like a glow-worm as it left his
   fingers;
Rumour had it that his name meant *harvester of wheat*.

When he took his secret departure, temples and shrines
Generated themselves from white threads in sepia
   memory,
Rising as mushrooms rise unplanned across the moist
   countryside,
And candles that guttered under limewashed domes were
   signs

Of an illumination that had not yet revealed
The witnesses to themselves, but existed like daylight
Or like the piping of leaf warblers hidden in woodland,
Directionless, meaning and whereabouts both concealed.

Looking over London

High, vibrating on its pillar of air,
An angel of death hovers like a kestrel
Above every dwelling, messuage and tenement,
Waiting for flash of is it heliograph
To stoop, strike hungrily and carry off.
Quarry clamped beneath talon, each can feed
Fragments of soul to its angel offspring.
So are the spiritual bodies reared.

A bitter image, do I hear you say,
Lifting your head from your platter of mutton?
But the muttons built themselves up on grass
Before you unsheathed your knife, and the grass
Lifted itself from fields of dust and dew
To meet those mechanically cropping lips.

On Top

For Liz

The mountain peak is bare, quite bare,
Snow in winter, wet rock in summer,
Affording no toe-hold for heather.
A few primitive forms of life,
Easily overlooked, hang on.
It is no place; when you arrive
There is nothing to do but die
Or depart, having left the mark
Of your hob-nailed presence by adding
Another blunt fragment of stone
To the poor attempt at a cairn.

On the uncommon days when cloud
Steams off to the bluish horizon,
You put names to parts of the vista,
Using words like Kerry and Cork
To plant your flag on indistinct
Slivers of olive, sage and buff,
Darker in tone than the enveloping
Air that blows white noise in your ear.

What might be a steeple reminds you
That people, assumed to be there
And infesting the land like mites,
Are busying themselves as ever
With God and his opposite number –
Who at least have the *savoir faire*
Never to manifest themselves
Up here on this unshapely crag.
It could be called a silver lining.

Whatever the prospect may offer,
It is not, repeat not, temptation.

In the valley below, a croak
And a black shape which you denote
By the substantive 'raven' drifts
With striking angular velocity
Across your visual field. Yes,
The sounds are of wind, raven, rush
Of breath and the internal scraping
Of scarlet blood driving through arteries.
Go heave a rock over the edge:
It goes bounding, knocking, rebounding
Off and down with fading concussions
Into the safety of the thalweg –
A grey horse in flight from demons.

The sun hovers over Cape Clear
And the spell of oneness is past.
Time now for the lopsided descent,
Slithering over unstable scree
To stumble on tufts of bog-cotton,
Skirting small Lake Acoose, whose waters,
Brown as an Egyptian eye, buoy up
Red-spotted trout that waver in neutral
Under spongy banks, unperturbed
By you and your dark glasses, knowing
You lack the rod, the skill, the will.

Firing

Around noon the artillery began
Excoriating the municipal good
With marigold bursts and puffs of surprise.
Soon it will be the turn of the villas.
Their lounges are waiting under closed eyelids,
Plastic albums pressed to their bosoms, albums
Of smiles, laughing mothers and aunts and boyfriends.
What was there to be so cheerful about –
Last month, even ten years ago, or ever?

I recall a forest fire, the real thing
Seen in the movies, and the shock of it –
The roar, the onrush of singed animals,
Silhouettes streaming past, leopard and herbivore
Hunted by furnace flame from hell's mouth.
Snakes were too slow, birds fell out of the smoke.

As always, safe conduct for fugitives
Turns on the whim of tornadoes, waltzing
Waywardly out of the possible futures
That group and regroup below the horizon.

Not for Transcription into Braille

Autumn forms itself from ochre pigment,
From umber November; oil-bound whites
And clays are mashed and puddled by spatula
For stiff froth of traveller's joy;
Dull vert of yew is the eye-catcher
In the grisaille and sienna woods.

Tell me when I may use the bright colours,
The unsqueezed tubes of cadmium red,
Peacock and emerald and lemon,
Let my eye move among flecks of chroma
Like an anteater's tongue among termites.
Fusillades that rattle on the retina.

Meantime I sit alone in my rib-cage
Staring out through my not-violet eyes
At the not-viridian sun descending
On serrated not-magenta conifers,
Beneath which nondescript rodents creep
Untroubled by my not-loving gaze.

From the North

A secret society of fungi
Is pushing up among pine needles,
Keeping itself to itself.
Overhead crossbills raid the cones,
And here is the troll, peregrinating
Through air scented with resin,
Swinging the traditional club
In hairy-backed, unmanicured hand,
Brown trilby tipped over the eyes,
Humming a snatch of *Finlandia*
Under inflammable breath.

From the forest with raised arm
As of one who tenders thanks
For applause pattered from gloved hands,
He whirls away, Gog in a taxi,
Away from doily-shaped snowflakes
Gusting over mica schist,
To a soft touch in the soft south,
And survives the hard passage,
The rock and smack of short seas
Coming up on windward bows,
Cracked skin stung by brine.

Legs wrapped in clouts against the damp
Carry him, taut with adrenalin,
Over or through the weak stockades.
But this is not Treasure Island.
In the valleys the smell of hogs
And recalcitrant peasants,
Elsewhere the wet wind in the trees

And salt water flooding the fens.
The streets are not paved, the lodes
That were spoken of are absent.
So much for the land of hope.

An opera uncurtains itself
And from home the soprano voices
Call to him in *Sprechgesang*
Across rows of forgetful heads.
But the cries fall short, mud-flats
And quicksands lie in wait,
On waste ground interlacing brambles
Hold up thorns to the clouds
While he stares over blanketed levels
And lacking a word for God,
Is unaware of His non-presence.

Shopping

My eye flits over the shelves of your shop,
Casting about for something to desire,
Halting at stoneware jars and moving on
To mouthfuls wrapped in vine-leaves, cans of soup,
Cheeses that smell like saints, yesterday's crop
Of field mushrooms with sepia gills – so many
Shades of taste that mesmerize and are gone.
Instead of the voluptuous I need
Pepper and chilli to disperse the haze
And twist the lens of the mind into focus.
Something goes on out there, beyond the bland
Messages of the pink and sweet and cool:
When the stung membranes have subsided, ways
Open within the neural calm disclosing
The silent flux of groundwater through sand.

Necropolis

Downstairs, among the assembled bones
Of Stegosaur and Megatherium
Third-year Primary are having fun.
Their passerine cries unzip
The Victorian groins and vaults.

Up here in the Gallery's galleries,
Vibrationless and unvisited,
Cliffs of mahogany cabinets
Hold sepulchres with floors of cork
For solitary bees and wasps,
Pinned through thorax, wings outstretched,
Each with an epitaph attached –
Latin name, date and place of death.
Ten thousand species, rank upon rank,
Impaled and rigid in a dark
Odour of creosote and cloves;
Not a massed formation frozen
In flight to the flowery meadows,
Nor soundless gathering-place
For small invertebrate ghosts,
Nor consecrated matrix
Of crosses in a field of war graves,
But relics of sacrifice
To Apollonian order.

Nearly closing time and, below,
The children have fluttered away
From the halls of the Mesozoic.
In the café, shrill voices rise
Above the bubbles of fizzy drinks.

Sodium Light

At night the honey-fungus takes over,
Cinnamon spores coat the roads and houses.
Zephyr comes to town as Typhoid Mary.

An ice-riddled gale birches the breakers
Up and over the old sea wall –
Swillings torn off a peat-stained bay.

Shop awnings flap like wounded pelicans.
At thump and crash and clatter of grapeshot
The Oasis Club twitches its curtains.

Inside, the 'Thunder and Lightning' polka
And the tape of Punjabi love-songs
Unwinding into the early hours.

And the bus-shelter has its tenant,
Aged Tweedledum, to whom low voices
Murmur about agents and radiation.

Peering from his castellated head,
The amber streetscape outmanoeuvres him
After the exodus of the residents.

Prayer-wheel

Your name rackets around in my prayer-wheel
In the winds that blow off the ice-sheet,
With your vital and mortal statistics,
Colour of hair, wet blackness of pupils,
Written in waterproof ink, and my
Best guess about your most private places.
There's even a sketch. That and the words
Seem to match my scumbled rememberings.

Hurrah for the efficacy of prayer.
So who is it standing on the threshold,
Is it real you or some female golem
Dreamed up in basements of the Staré Město,
Contrived and released on me by one
Who sits on a dusty velvet cushion
Where a feeble filament makes legible
Scripts held inches from his skinny nose?

Or have I been dealt the House of God?
Wearing your features, does some poor imbecile
Tack towards me in a private storm
Across a sea of tarmac, shouting
Blurred senseless words, expecting an answer?
The obedient prayer-wheel spins and conjures,
Rattling mindlessly on in the Arctic
Wind that whistles to itself through its teeth.

Aside

The liver-coloured dog halts and looks up
Through the one-way mirror of his pale eyes
And writes me off. Also the strutting man
With the nightstick and dark, sun-flashing glasses,
He sees me as one to be disregarded.
Descending from the promenade, I walk
The beach in my helmet of invisibility.
Inland, the woods harbour exclusive birds
Whose utterances pass over my head.

Difficult not to scold at all these beings
Who sense that one does not figure in their futures.
So get on with it, but do not look to me
When black helicopters are beating the air
And their down-draught scatters your wits like chaff,
Or the looters swarm through the old town
With stones and petrol. Curled up in my form,
I hold my breath as uncountable hooves
Drum across a summer-hardened savannah.

Thoughts Slide out of Thoughts

Thoughts slide out of thoughts, like an old brass telescope,
Lubricated with ambiguity, bent by time.

The past oozes up through the pores of the present:
In a cliff-face near Lyme Regis, say the textbooks,
Plates of shale glisten with oil rendered and pressed
Out of the segmented bodies of the Triassic.

And the voice of Yeats, with his forced incantation
Pitched above the hiss of the nineteen-thirties —
A stag beetle in flight, wavering at sundown
Over thorn trees set up before a cyclorama —
Uttering fought-for words into a machine's ear:
Words pressed upon words to drip aromatic oil.

Likewise bubbles in Baltic amber enclose
Air exhaled by mammoths, even by troglodytes
Hunted or hunting on feet bundled in rawhide,
Quartering their woods for game and tribal enemies,

Moving onwards as we all move, incontinently,
Sliding into the future down muddy tracks.

Wall of Death, Bray

Lashing out with my celluloid windmill
At the stuffed finch fastened to a hat
And at giant legs trousered in twill,
Shod in oppressor's brogues, I disowned
Their covenants and allegiances.

Let me stand outside the Wall of Death
Where the blonde woman in riding breeches
Straddles and revs up her scarlet bike.
(From her companion, the lean-jawed man
With a cowlick, I avert my thoughts.)

Later, from within, the roar of engines
Rises to frenzy and the hooped timber
Cylinder shudders under the rite –
Hidden from me where I hang around,
Learning, as always, only from hearsay.

History

Through ragged breakers landing
On cobble beachhead fighting
On sugar-soft strand escaping
From corn-brash cliff-tops watching
By hovel doorways gaping
In narrow chapels praying
At sodden gravesides standing

By market-cross decreeing
In hatchet tongues condemning
With chains and nooses humbling
To murrain lands expelling
On tares and tillage stumbling
To rat's disease succumbing
From past and pasture fleeing

In killjoy keeps despairing
By land-locked manors idling
With pin-sharp spires astounding
To pipe and tabor dancing
Through game-rich forests hounding
In unclipped coinage hoarding
Of old heart-grief uncaring

Flies and Nettles

The purpose of nettles is to make more nettles,
green, bitter, sharply hairy and introverted,
and they in turn shall make yet more nettles,
and so on, until the land is nettle-cloaked.

From a space station it might look like green baize.

Ditto for flies; the air will be full of flies;
and the green baize will not be seen by the astronauts
because of all the flies that are in between.

And mankind will live between the flies and nettles.

When men have poisoned the nettles and the flies,
the granular skin of the earth will be visible,
but not for long, because the people will breed
and encrust the land like a swarm of locusts.

Then people crowded upon demented people
will succumb to their poisons, and once again
the earth will be brown and bare, or nearly so –
for the torpid roots will be stirring themselves
and flies will crawl on stiff legs out of their silos.

Soon the land will again be coated in nettles,
stinging the flesh that strokes them, and all the air
will vibrate to the incessant humming of the flies.

Big Cat

Here is the pelt, yellow and flexible,
Poured out like soup on the plank floor,
Bodiless and shampooed by furrier
To exorcize dreams of carnivore.

Ants in their dry galleries
Sensing honey on the wind
File out to invade the carcass
This softly hairy skin defended.

I wrap it round my bony shoulders
And crouch in the fork of a tree
While cogitating on salvation,
The failure of the rains and sweetness.

Montages

The tin-dredger grumbles in the forest;
In a brown river brown men and boys
Slick palmolive soap between pale palms
While cook prepares the peppery dinner:

Down in Wairakei flowers of sulphur
Colour the rocks where steam-vents and fumaroles
Roar round the clock, and the cheap hotels
Boast of double-glazing in their bedrooms:

Guiding hands; the planchette spells out *kiosk*:
And a crow, no it's really a lapwing,
Is buffeting the air among grey
Skeletons of what once were elm trees:

Four images spilled from the psyche;
Mercury from a broken thermometer,
Bright globules escaping into crannies
And a dry stalk left between clumsy fingers.

Perhaps *Khios* is what was intended?
Khios with Homeric crags and groves
Of lentisk, and a Japanese truck
Trundling the mastic down to the quayside:

Plastic bottles bobbing on the waves
Of the Aegean, on the chaotic
Frontier that divides breathing from drowning –
Yes, *chaos* was the word, and the word

In Hartslock Wood

CAROLINE IS A PRAT: graffito chalked
On a green-streaked concrete pill-box
Run up against the clock in 1940,
Hemmed in later by a henge of beeches
Standing at attention in mouldy silence.
Scenery set, a stage prepared, a crib
For heroism and funk to be born into,
Now a repository for crumpled cans,
Condoms and faeces. But well made,
It will see out Berkshire's bricks and tiles.
Archaeologists to come will ruminate
On this cheerless dwelling of the natives
At the turn of the second millennium –
Just about the time of the final break-up
(According to their finical monographs).

What the Wild Waves Say

Over cornfields shunned by harvester and rook
Helicopters hustle the gun-laden nouns,
Adjectives circulate counterfeit currency,
A suburb straddled by clauses has the look

Of a zone marked down for righteous liberation.
The refugees' lorries have run out of rhetoric,
Irregular verbs are mining the bridges
And barbed syntax shields the television station.

The realm is laid waste, but supplies of words
Find their way to the sunburned frontline Mercuries,
Below whose crisp voices runs the ground-bass
Of augurs interpreting the flight of birds.

Genealogy

Those whom you pursue
Were not the stocky dark-haired ones
(They went to the wall
Or more likely over the cliffs)
Nor the blunt-headed heavyweights,
Lamented arrivals,
But coming in between from marshland
Dolichocephalics
Nondescript in the mass but able,
Hot-tempered ousters later ousted,
Conquerors, then conquered.

In old age ninety generations
Is a distance just within grasping.
What links with whom are you in need of?
Would it discount your unimportance
To be sure your genes
Or some of them in first editions
Had gone to earth between stone slabs,
A long barrow, a lapsing hummock
In a pasture of rank cocksfoot
Spattered with cow-dung,
With the midges endlessly
Whirling over snuff-coloured pools?

Or would you find it more affecting
If the carrier of those genes
That shaped your ear-lobes
Had been a rallier of rebels,
A raiser of hope in the dispossessed,
Who then shouted and lunged with pikes

In backyards and alleyways,
All of them ending on the gallows?

Or had landlorded it in gaiters
Over Munster acres,
Half-fuddled with alcohol,
While above in a chilly bedroom
In a cursive hand
A maiden lady wrote a novel,
Long, heartfelt and stilted,
Seen by none but a female cousin,
Barely skimmed by her?

But the tree needs pruning.
Those who are only names on gravestones
And the meanly wicked,
Unlucky or soft in the head
Are subjects for you on your ladder
Wielding the secateurs and culling
Twigs to make a bonfire.
And the smoke elevates itself
Among the acceptable branches,
And the steel-ruled sunlight
Grey on grey picks out
The seedlings that shoot from the humus.

Pantomime

Flooded in lilac light the awaited fairy,
Esmeralda, pin-points across the stage,
Chin uplifted, her smile sweet and remote
Far from the silk-clad thighs below her tutu,
Briefly touching with diamanté wand
The warm fontanelle of her doting page.

But who is it with twitching palps that scuttles
In the dark hinterland, spying from coverts,
Who, caught by the green spotlight, howls with rage,
Radiating malice (absurd but scary) –
And, pierced by the hero's glittering rapier,
Dies and endows the lovers with his hunger?

A Samaritan Surprised

Hewing and thrusting through the scrub,
    Grasped at by strangling figs,
Shouldered by dipterocarps, impaled
    On spiny palms, I came
To a man-made absence of trees.
    Parting the fronds I peered
At a bare podsol-floored arena
    In which I saw a man,
Naked, bound tightly to a post
    And moaning through his gag.
Just two of us, one free, one captive,
    Hearing the bell-like cries
Of unconcerned and unseen birds
    High in the dripping canopy.

I without thinking forced my way
    Into the green-walled clearing
And ran – a dozen leaping steps –
    To cut the victim free.
But as I reached the stake, in tumult
    Men of all sizes broke
Shouting from the sheltering forest,
    Gesturing with machetes,
And seized me roughly, held me down,
    Intimidating me
With incomprehensible threats.
    Just as they bore me off,
On the refracting edge of vision,
    I saw the seeming prisoner
Slip free his wrists, quickly unwind
    The cords I thought so fast

And merge into the howling troupe.
    Did I – or was it fancy? –
Glimpse the forerunner of a grin
    Flicker below his features?

Fearful, carried by twisting footways
    Cut through the bush, we reached
A hunter's hut, dim, thatched and smoky,
    Set between buttressed trees;
Inside they threw me on a mattress
    Of dusty leaves and skins.
And then, as if a lamp had bloomed,
    The scowls and anger vanished,
Replaced by whoops of laughter, gleeful
    Contortions, tears of mirth.
Gently, with reassuring smiles,
    They set me on my feet.
Women arrived with pots of stew,
    We ate, and from a gourd
I drank some stinging liquor, braved
    The bizarre hilarity,
Saw moving lights, stumbled and slept.

    I woke alone with visions
Flying like bats inside my skull
    While pain surged in my bowels.
Out of control, invading words,
    Images, arrows, fragments,
Flashed and sieved through my mind like shoals
    Of krill and silver smelt
Through a spreadeagled net. For days,
    Night after night, I groaned,
Feeling myself observed by something
    Among the cobwebbed rafters

That hung head down and never stirred
    But crepitated dryly.

When time no longer moved, a stranger
    Speaking my language came,
Raised me from where I lay inert
    In fetid pools and darkness,
And with a case of foreign medicines
    Healed me, restored my strength.
Venturing out, we scraped through leafage
    That overgrew a world
Of stridulating insects, slashed
    At thorny growths and branches,
Arduously steering for safety.
    But from dense jungle burst
A roar of maledictory voices,
    And the same savage men
Brushing aside the dangling epiphytes
    Raged wildly out to take us.
I fled and hid, but looking back
    Saw carried off unconscious,
Bound with lianas, my true doctor.

Sleep

Two pedals, one to go faster, one slower –
And a third for disconnecting the mind
From the streamers and quills and crying music.
Even to this tenth-floor bedroom the wind

Brings dust and grumbling from the bauxite mills,
And from the street, yelps of what could be pleasure
Or pain. Tonight may the third pedal save me
From the streamers and crying music and quills.

Night terrors get a mention in the textbooks.
So I, from the airless space-time of dreamers,
Break surface, splashing, to seize the handrail
Of the crying music and quills and streamers.

Konzertstück

The fiddlers' fingers stamp on the strings,
Rise and fall again, wave like pale claws
Of crabs on the mud-flats of Guyana.

But the sweating conductor is bee-like,
Dances *à la* von Frisch on his podium,
Bobs, half-gyrates, tells with his antenna

The whereabouts of the fields of honey —
South-eastward, just as far as it takes
Schubert to make landfall and cast anchor.

Revelations

The sermon in the Deer Park
The entry into Jerusalem
The migration to Medina –
All samples of the story-teller's repertoire.
Now they call for a new story
An epiphany unthought-of
A vehement creed announcing
Release for them, confinement for the rest.

But who is this story-teller
The spell-binding mythopoeist?
All we want is a straight answer.
Why are we fobbed off, dazzled and distracted
With miracles and enigmas
Effigies masked to the eyeballs
In silver, breeze-tinkled bells –
A string of coloured balls across the pram?

With ideas above their station
Corpuscles question the heart
Unable to comprehend
Replies delivered in a higher tongue.
Circles of zeal expand
Bluebottles rage at the window
And the believer's lamp
Burns high in dephlogisticated air.

Country and Town

Barking of tethered dogs,
Dead jays and magpies nailed
Bedraggled on a fence,
Grain for ripening pheasants.
A rubber-booted figure
Slouches across the yard
With a pail of sour swill
To tip into the piggery;
Curses the dogs, returns.
Out of the swinging door
A yelp of beaten music
Breaks loose, bolts like a convict
Into impartial woodland,
Where the rain dribbles down
On a derelict telly
And a stained lilac mattress
Not quite hidden by nettles.

One vintage port, an Armagnac for my friend,
And ask the porter if he'd call a cab
To get me to the ten-fifteen at Paddington.
Where were we? yes, you'd like a little shooting –
What shall we say – the weekend after next?

Reading Time

A differed from B in shape and sound,
Or so ran tiresome theory; what mattered
Was the great goal – books before my eyes,
Stories and verses infilling silence.

Near the beginning of Chapter One,
In faint pencil, mother underlined
The words of two syllables or more.
Then each sentence was an enterprise.
Attention could slip; long days divided
Accessible 'also' on page eight
From the sophisticated 'although'
Two pages later.

     Things speeded up
With the chemical trance of puberty.
On a stage lit by fanciful novels
Intrigues advanced through tiny events
To bliss and desolation and back.

The current of fiction quickened, time
Took to the air, single peaks swept by,
Only the toothed ranges, mauve and white,
Cut recoverable tracks in memory.

The first decade, when books came one by one,
Was in itself a library of years.
By pension time, with shelves stiffly packed
And books reclining on books upstanding,
One bestseller symbolized twelve months
Of time the dimension, not time reading –

With the short story a later image.
Finally a blur of turning leaves.

This was true, I think, for my mother, who
In her last months laid aside her paperback
And looked quietly out at timelessness.

II

A Tropical Caress

Cardiac music over all –
The sea, the shelly sand, the rocks –
Bleeds from a stationary car.

Silent among the dozing palms,
Two (to be lovers), linking, thinking,
Advance upon the littoral.

To him then for consideration:
Downswept hair, and upswept neck
Stemming from naked shoulder;

And tinted mouth from which issues
Small sophisticated bird-voice;
And rustle of accoutrements.

Now music is truly background;
A species of desire affects
The singer in the shiny box.

Turning at tideline, face to face,
The endearments flag – and could
They? Yes probably, yes, they think

That not impossible and
(Stand clear of the irony)
Kiss, kiss in the warm latitude.

Descending

Ivy's body was firm and warm, Emma's was soft and cool,
And whichever I clasped, it was always the other I wanted;
But then I was young and the waters above my head
Were green with the light of something called the sun.

Next there was Fay, with a mole like the map of Ireland
Which could only be seen by those in the orchestra stalls,
And Lottie with curly hair between her breasts
Who could make me feel that my world was upside down;

Amy was eager (like a snake's her tongue), and Ingrid
Was an equable philosophe who smelt of sun-dried hay —
But these were in twilight, twilit depths; and now it's you
Offering asylum between resilient thighs.

But my feet are weighted with time, and I sink in solitude
To black levels where the sea is cold and still,
Where demonic fish with phosphorescent gee-gaws
Twist and flick past me, mouthing words I cannot hear.

Is There Life on Venus?

Somebody's rounded biscuit-coloured girl
Waits affably in that amazing car –
Which shines with emblems and whose one small dent
On the almost esculent envelope
Is evidence perhaps of asteroid.

Enclosed by tinted glass and stroked with music,
Functional disorder a fret unknown,
She smokes, skims through expensive magazines
(Too dear, alas, for us), switches adroitly
Her disposition of desirable legs.

Existing, you see, on a plane completely other
– Even her vowels are slightly beyond our reach –
Like a subversive ideogram, she sits
Poised in this would-be interplanetary machine,
Awaiting her lover (from whom may Heaven defend us).

Washington DC, 1964

A Suit of Armour

When hares were caught by stableboys with bells
And saints journeyed with eyes reversed in prayer,
When chivalrous men with servants were depicted
Disporting on a flowered field of gold,
This nasty contrivance was all too often seen
Being galloped about by some long-suffering horse.

Herzmund ('Baron') was inside, lapped in sweat.
Flexing the hinged and riveted shell, he peered
For prey through slits above an iron snout.
At night – the takings tossed into a chest –
He dined grossly and aired his views on death
While someone helpless screamed in a deep basement.

Charming vignette; but why, you say, be morbid?
Consider the craftsmanship, the Vulcan skill,
The arabesques engraved on the cuirass,
The nimble patterns – and the entertaining
Protection provided for the Baron's genitals;
Think of it, if you like, as abstract sculpture.

Quite; but I think mainly of the confronted
Traveller impaled by terror or in earnest,
The mounted devil-dress glimpsed in the gloaming,
The cornering and the wordless savagery.
Yes, hung in public, armour is fair monument
For those who see if not for those who look.

The Musical Lover

The hall, the crowd, the orchestra in action,
Swirling traffic of themes and chords directed
By a famous figure in tails and, absent
Among his metaphors, my lurking listener.
The music stopped, the drums filled up with silence,
Then cataracts of mad applause collapsed
On his image-full word-forsaken head.
Hastily out with him (clap clap beclapping),
Running down stone steps (clap fainter beclapped),
Escaping through stale ochre-painted passages
Into the sky-roofed anechoic night.

But now the immense emotional sphere –
All incandescence, indigo and portents –
Paled and dwindled, angels turned pedestrian,
Flowers and feelings sank to monochrome
And magic returned to the buzzing jungle.
Pushing away anxiety, he thought
(To use an old-fashioned phrase) of his mistress,
Long-legged and loving in a one-room lodging,
And the lights rose again in his mind's theatre.

Neither blanched northern witch nor generalized
Odalisque, but the unique girl's image
Now extended her arms behind his eyes.
So the deafening city was endurable,
Being occulted, no roars of approval
Hounded the harmony, and his back shivered
At the memory of her stroking nails.

This pair had once made love upon a hill-top
When breezes breathing fitfully through heather
Were background to the self-communing solo
Of a foraging bee; and when a curlew
Cried a reminder of their solitudes.

Years on, encrusted with events, his vision
Self-pleasingly twisted to aberration,
The strings and horns may lull him to accept

Being one among many isolations.

Kostchei

Hiding in the garden of Kostchei's palace,
Hearing cries between ecstasy and anguish,
Jangling of iron chains, hyaena malice,
Plucked music and horns, we meet, not to languish

(We who have not succumbed), like the enchanted
Who face their faceless tantalizers, dying
Daily, and are Kostchei's treasure; but granted
We escape, to love. Why then are we sighing?

Our embraces slacken, weathercocks veer,
Thin smoke blows past us and a drum-beat begs
For the resolution of fear, and here
Creeps the arthritic king on rigid legs.

Hurrying apart, we weep, claims overthrown,
And as we entered so we leave, alone.

Elegy for Faustina

Faustina, if that was your name, you are dead,
And your beauty, which sculptors hinted at in stone
And poets expanded their language to render in words,
Is less than a cobweb in a scholar's mind.
And now I (how foolish it sounds) feel for you something –
At all costs let us not call it love.

But there are nights when instead of sleeping I think of you
And lie feverishly awake on knives of roses,
And as it were through a crack in an embankment
Besieging sorrow enters, and ridiculous tears
Exude from my prosaic mud-coloured eyes.
Later I sleep, dreaming perhaps of streets and buses.

Or in the sunlight, walking through the streets,
My tie neatly knotted and my hair smoothed down,
To all appearances like someone in his senses,
There are days when it seems you are continually present
And I think of your cream-coloured body, your carmine
    lips
And your impossible pride (for that I blame your parents).

But each time, as though through depths of glass, I see you
Surrounded by netted birds and captured lovers,
I remember today's ruin which tourists yawn at
Was the temple where self-consuming candles flared,
That Venus was someone important when you were young
And the fixed stars were fixed in different places.

The Assassination

The great hall empty and the porters God knows where,
The brilliant street, seen through the colonnade, deserted,
And stillness, silence, except for some distant shouting:
What has happened? What is it all about? What's up?

Dust still hangs in the air, someone inside a house
Closes the shutters violently on the white street,
Bolts are shot, the faces of the houses are blank,
Giving away nothing of what has just occurred.

But there (over there) is blood on the gritty road
And spattered on the steps of an important building.
Safety is short of breath, explanations and fear
Uncoil themselves in the trembling air. Bells strike the
    hour,

The roar of the crowd grows louder – and I look guilty
Lurking alone beside the spot marked with an X
To possible watchers concealed by curtained windows.
I must leave, go slowly, unconcernedly saunter,

Move imperceptibly away through narrow streets
And avoid the Square where news goes up like a rocket,
Where the mad mob, its huge heart pounding like an
    engine,
Sighting a lonely stranger, may effect its felony.

Twice this year for this reason I have skulked in shelter
And made my way home later through the moonlit town,
Thinking that despite tomorrow's revenge and curfews
The great eagles would soon be extinct in this country.

Townsman in the Country

Can he have disregarded all these nights
Her invitation, her implicit presence,
Have ignored or misunderstood the trees
Signalling wildly from a windy ridge?
What can justify his nocturnal tremor,
The attention he pays to minute noises,
Creatures abroad, the leaves requesting silence?
What does he think is walking on the roof?
To what conclusion was he led at nightfall,
Hearing a small scream issue from a wood?
What lies behind his nonchalant departure,
His travel to the place where she is not?
Can he feel glad in his electric city,
Safer among his engines and his shadows?

First-born

For Mary

Welcome to the lascivious Court of Wei
   With the clamour of coloured rattles,
With crackers banging in the boisterous street
And saffron kites exalted in a gay sky.
     Returning from their battles,
    It's you the quilted soldiers greet.

In the towns shouting, in the villages dancing –
   They rejoice with percussive hymns
While intricate compliments and silks are borne
From our raffish prince to you: and here comes, prancing
     On his magical limbs,
    The prayed-for, peaceful unicorn.

In the Tower

This old armour, shown now in a glass case,
Was designed by a master of alarm.
Here, in a mature vision of malevolence,
He gave shape to the implacable inflictor
Who, on byways of pilgrimage, clashed out
From wailing spinneys to project his rage.

Help was away where, bland beside a wheatfield,
A hunting baron paused for pies and wine.

The Exile

Low in the west, I watch myself in motion
And laugh to see an exiled king surviving
Upheld by cliffs above a heaving ocean,

Lodged in ruins where Atlantic rains, driving
Unchecked across nude limestone acres, humble
His eighty years, absolve the will from striving.

Gales blow up from the west, the wave-tops crumble
In spray, shatter on cliffs, their form and action
Lost in tumult where sea-birds dive and tumble.

Revolution revealed the faithful faction
Who brought me (trembling) to this eagle's station
And strain to succour me, Virtue's exaction.

The red-hot sun descends, a nightmare nation
Surges through sleep to mimic my disaster –
New memories, not of my own creation.

The mob shouts and inciting drums beat faster,
The rumble and tread draws near, cries for slaughter
Sound while they burn effigies of their master.

I see a roof in flames, wild without water,
Wild men storming a gateway, leagued for plunder
And hear the sobbing of my ravished daughter.

Then flight across the plains to seas which sunder
King from kingdom and cockatoo from raven;
A frail smack carried me to the waves' thunder,

To a landing of sad flotsam in craven
Darkness (falling on the cliff path, wind whipping
Words away), to life on this black-faced haven.

These islands . . . this seaboard is shunned by shipping;
Events pass overhead like clouds to scatter
Fortune and rain on foreign mountains, gripping

Cities with hope or fear. Winter storms batter
And undermine my cliffs. My servants – lowly,
Hankering for a restoration – chatter

About miracles, something strange and holy.
All weakness, dreamers' nonsense, a fool's notion.
Fire destroyed my home, my asylum slowly
Falls to the consuming, wave-ridden ocean.

The Seven Banquets

Verses for an illuminated manuscript

One summer evening on the palace roof
  In seven pavilions caged,
To entertain an ancient lonely king
  Seven strange feasts were staged.

The first was queened by Silence, clocks stood still,
  Mandolins lay unplucked,
While infants from the breasts of comely nurses
  Luxuriously sucked.

Schoolboys in riot, hot with seasoned meat,
  The second banquet lorded,
Shouted and wrestled in the gorgeous room
  That king and Time accorded.

Flowering lovers feasted in the third,
  Hand intertwined with hand,
Their thoughts as one, spellbound by Her whose love
  Unnumbered men outmanned.

Next were the rattling military, boastful,
  Drunk on an even keel,
Inventing the past with a scarlet gesture
  And clink of formal steel.

Judges like Jupiters firm-lipped and paunchy
  Sat before plates of gold,
Debated and sipped and sombrely, gravely
  In legal orbits rolled.

Unhungry fading scholars watched the growth
  Of shadows on the lawn,

Their grand climacteric's falling graph
  On parchment faces drawn.

Great age was in the last; pain made some fretful,
  Weakness made others weep,
Those who could laugh laughed softly; those who could
                                  hear
  A string band lulled to sleep.

The king observed each feast, smiles on his lips
  And eagles in his eyes,
But was not, when his guests had gone away,
  Less lonely or more wise.

A Meeting on Gold Leaf

The king is promenading by
A castle on the sward,
Crown on his head, his velvet cloak
Held by a silken cord;

His formal gardens peopled by
Peacock and tufted crane,
An elkhound stalking at his side
Leashed on a silver chain.

Scent of jasmine and treble voice
Foretell the queen's approach –
Rustle of silk (but soundless step),
Glimmer of crystal brooch.

Natural music fills her ear
By hidden finches played,
And cedars from the burning sun
Her inbred beauty shade.

Forests of faith and errantry,
Magpie and soothing dove,
Witness and guard their meeting and
Their colloquy of love.

III

The Fall

The Garden of Eden (described in the Bible)
Was Guinness's Brewery (mentioned by Joyce),
Where innocent Adam and Eve were created
And dwelt from necessity rather than choice;

For nothing existed but Guinness's Brewery,
Guinness's Brewery occupied all,
Guinness's Brewery everywhere, anywhere –
Woe that expulsion succeeded the Fall!

The ignorant pair were encouraged in drinking
Whatever they fancied whenever they could,
Except for the porter or stout which embodied
Delectable knowledge of Evil and Good.

In Guinness's Brewery, innocent, happy,
They tended the silos and coppers and vats,
They polished the engines and coopered the barrels
And even made pets of the Brewery rats.

One morning while Adam was brooding and brewing
It happened that Eve had gone off on her own,
When a serpent like ivy slid up to her softly
And murmured seductively, Are we alone?

O Eve, said the serpent, I beg you to sample
A bottle of Guinness's excellent stout,
Whose nutritive qualities no one can question
And stimulant properties no one can doubt;

It's tonic, enlivening, strengthening, heartening,
Loaded with vitamins, straight from the wood,
And further enriched with the not undesirable
Lucrative knowledge of Evil and Good.

So Eve was persuaded and Adam was tempted,
They fell and they drank and continued to drink
(Their singing and dancing and shouting and prancing
Prevented the serpent from sleeping a wink).

Alas, when the couple had finished a barrel
And swallowed the final informative drops,
They looked at each other and knew they were naked
And covered their intimate bodies with hops.

The anger and rage of the Lord were appalling,
He wrathfully cursed them for taking to drink
And hounded them out of the Brewery, followed
By beetles (magenta) and elephants (pink).

The crapulous couple emerged to discover
A universe full of diseases and crimes,
Where porter could only be purchased for money
In specified places at specified times.

And now in this world of confusion and error
Our only salvation and hope is to try
To threaten and bargain our way into Heaven
By drinking the heavenly Brewery dry.